T0402421

ARE THEY REAL?

ESP

by Carla Mooney

BrightP★int Press

San Diego, CA

© 2024 BrightPoint Press
an imprint of ReferencePoint Press, Inc.
Printed in the United States

For more information, contact:
BrightPoint Press
PO Box 27779
San Diego, CA 92198
www.BrightPointPress.com

LIBRARY OF CONGRESS CATALOGING-IN-PUBLICATION DATA

Names: Mooney, Carla, 1970--author.
Title: ESP / by Carla Mooney.
Other titles: Extrasensory perception
Description: San Diego, CA: BrightPoint Press, [2024] | Series: Are they real? | Includes
    bibliographical references and index. | Audience: Ages 13 | Audience: Grades 7-9
Identifiers: LCCN 2023012468 (print) | LCCN 2023012469 (eBook) | ISBN 9781678206260
    (hardcover) | ISBN 9781678206277 (eBook)
Subjects: LCSH: Extrasensory perception--Juvenile literature. | Parapsychology--Juvenile
    literature.
Classification: LCC BF1321 .M66 2024 (print) | LCC BF1321 (eBook) | DDC 133.8--dc23/
    eng/20230415
LC record available at https://lccn.loc.gov/2023012468
LC eBook record available at https://lccn.loc.gov/2023012469

CONTENTS

AT A GLANCE

- Humans have five senses. They are sight, hearing, smell, touch, and taste. Extrasensory perception (ESP) is the ability to sense more than that. It is called the sixth sense.

- ESP covers a range of abilities, including precognition, telepathy, and clairvoyance.

- Precognition is the ability to know that something is going to happen before it does. Telepathy means that someone can read minds. Clairvoyance is the ability to see people, objects, or events that are far away.

- Parapsychology is the study of ESP.

- The US government researched ESP in Project Star Gate between the 1970s and 1990s. The military tried to use ESP to gather intelligence.

- Evidence for ESP includes personal accounts and experiences. Some scientific studies have also shown evidence of ESP.

- Daryl Bem is a scientist who published an important study on ESP in 2011.

- Some scientists have tried to redo earlier studies on ESP. They don't always find the same results. Other scientists say that the evidence for ESP isn't very strong.

- ESP has been the subject of books, movies, and television shows. Reality shows feature mediums communicating with spirits of the dead.

- About 35 percent of adults in the United States believe that ESP abilities exist.

INTRODUCTION

A PREMONITION OF DISASTER

O n July 17, 1981, Jean Sternecker and her husband, Robert, were on a date night. They went to a dance at the Hyatt Regency hotel in Kansas City, Missouri. More than 1,600 people were there. Jean and Robert danced and had fun with friends.

Skywalks stretched high across the hotel lobby. The skywalks looked like floating bridges. They were the hotel's most interesting features. That evening, about sixty people gathered on the skywalks.

The Hyatt Regency had skywalks on the second, third, and fourth floors of the hotel.

They watched people dancing in the lobby below.

Jean and Robert were in the lobby. Suddenly, Jean had a strong feeling that something bad was about to happen. "The best way I can describe it is to say a voice came over me, saying 'Run, Jean, run.' It was inside me, but it was commanding," she said.[1] Jean jumped up. She grabbed her husband. She screamed at him to run.

A few seconds later, two skywalks crashed to the lobby floor. Hundreds of people were trapped. The deadly disaster killed 114 people. It injured 200 more.

Premonitions can take the form of sudden bad feelings, voices, or visions.

The Sterneckers were lucky. They had been sitting underneath the skywalks before they ran. Jean's **premonition** saved their lives.

A SPECIAL SENSE

Jean Sternecker does not know how she sensed that the Hyatt disaster was about to happen. Some people insist there must be an explanation. She must have noticed signs of the disaster to come. Maybe she heard a cracking noise. Maybe she noticed the skywalks moving. But other people believe the answer is something else. They think Jean's experience can be explained by a special sense called extrasensory perception (ESP).

Humans have five main senses. They are sight, hearing, smell, touch, and taste.

People say they must concentrate deeply to access their sixth sense.

ESP is known as the sixth sense. People with ESP can notice things around them that others cannot. Their experiences do not have a clear scientific explanation. For those who believe in ESP, these abilities might seem **paranormal**. But does ESP really exist?

1

WHAT IS ESP?

Some people claim they can see what is going to happen before it does. Others say they can communicate with the dead. Some people might even think they can read minds. These experiences may seem strange and creepy. Most people explain them as luck or **coincidences**. But some people call such events examples of ESP.

People gather information about the world around them through their five basic senses. People with ESP know more than what their eyes, ears, and noses can sense.

Some people use tools to make their ESP stronger.

ESP is the ability to sense information with the mind. Unlike physical senses, ESP works across very long distances. ESP can even reach forward or backward in time.

A RANGE OF ABILITIES

Many different abilities are all called ESP. Some people claim to have more than one type of ESP. People often experience ESP through visions, dreams, thoughts, and feelings.

One type of ESP is precognition. Precognition is the ability to see the future. This ability does not cause an event to happen. It allows a person to know about future events before they occur. One example of precognition took place in a Welsh village called Aberfan. In 1966, a deadly landslide killed nearly 150 people. The night before the disaster, an eight-year-old boy drew a picture. The boy's

DÉJÀ VU

Many people have experiences where they feel like they are living a moment again. They might believe that they can predict what is going to happen next. This is called déjà vu. Scientists say that déjà vu might happen because of connections inside the brain. These connections make an event feel familiar, even if it isn't.

picture showed many people digging on a hill. He wrote the words *the end* on the drawing. The next day, the boy died in the landslide. His drawing might have been a premonition about the tragedy.

People who predict the future are called psychics. Some psychics use special tools to help them see the future. These include **tarot cards** and crystal balls. Psychics might also read the lines on people's palms. Others read a person's energy to predict future events. This is also called reading a person's aura.

Palm reading can be used to predict how long people will live, what relationships they will have, how much money they will make, and more.

A related ESP ability is retrocognition. Retrocognition is the ability to see into the past. People claim to use retrocognition to see events that happened long ago. They might also see people and places from the past. These things appear as if they are in the present.

TELEPATHY

Telepathy is another type of ESP. Telepathy is the ability to read minds. It can be as simple as sensing another person's emotions. Or a telepathic person can be powerful enough to read someone's thoughts and memories. Two people might even be able to communicate without talking. Instead, they use only their minds. Twins sometimes seem to do this. It is called twin telepathy. Many twins say they

Many twins say they can communicate without talking. This ability isn't always considered telepathy, but some people believe that it is.

can feel their twins' emotions. Sometimes, twins say one can physically feel what is happening to the other.

Twins Gemma and Leanne Houghton believe that telepathy saved Leanne's life. One day, Gemma had a strong feeling that Leanne needed help. Leanne was taking a bath. "I just got this feeling to check on her, so I went up to the bathroom, and she was under the water," Gemma said.[2] Gemma pulled Leanne out of the water. She called for help. Gemma's actions saved her sister's life.

CLAIRVOYANCE

Some people report being able to see objects, people, or events that are far away. This ability is called clairvoyance. A man named Ingo Swann claimed to be clairvoyant. He could describe a location if he was given its **coordinates**. He could describe many details about places he had

ESP POTENTIAL

Some believers say that only certain people have ESP. They can use ESP only when they are in a special mental state. Other people think that everyone has the potential for ESP. Some people may be more in touch with their sixth sense than others.

never been. He said he could see these places in his mind.

A medium is a person who uses ESP to communicate with the spirits of the dead. Some mediums see spirits. Others receive messages from spirits through feelings or sensations. Some mediums allow spirits to use the medium's body to deliver messages. For example, a spirit might speak through a medium. The spirit could use the medium to send a message to loved ones.

Some people with ESP can touch a physical object and see images of a person

Mediums may use old belongings or photos to connect with a person's spirit.

or place. By touching the object, people can see how it was used in the past. They see events where the object was present. For example, a psychic might touch a missing person's clothing. The psychic can then see the person and know where the person can be found.

23

2

THE HISTORY OF ESP

People throughout history have believed in visions of the future. Many cultures have stories about communication with spirits. Some religious beliefs have things in common with ESP. In many cultures, these beliefs are still held today. But belief in the paranormal isn't only connected to specific religions and cultures.

SPIRITUALISM AND SÉANCES

In the 1800s, spiritualism became popular in the United States and Europe. Spiritualism is the belief that the spirits of the dead can be contacted. Some people held séances in

Séances have been recorded for hundreds of years. For many of these rituals, people gather around a table to call on a spirit.

their homes. A séance is a meeting led by a medium. The medium tries to contact the spirit of someone who has died.

By the late 1800s, scientists interested in spiritualism formed research societies. In 1882, the Society for Psychical Research was formed in London, England. In 1885, a

ABRAHAM LINCOLN'S DREAM

In April 1865, President Abraham Lincoln dreamed about a funeral. In the dream, he asked a soldier who had died. The soldier said it was the president. He had been killed by an assassin. Lincoln woke up and felt upset. Three days later, Lincoln was assassinated. His dream could be called a premonition.

similar group called the American Society for Psychical Research started in the United States. These societies were created to study spirits. They also investigated other forms of ESP. They gathered information and studied reports of ESP.

PARAPSYCHOLOGY RESEARCH

The study of ESP is called parapsychology. Some parapsychology research shows evidence of ESP. But many of the studies reveal that ESP abilities can be faked. Some scientists say the results proving ESP is real are explained by chance.

British researcher William Barrett conducted some of the first ESP studies in 1881. Barrett studied the five Creery sisters. The sisters said they could use telepathy. Barrett tested their claims. He sent one sister out of the room. Then Barrett wrote the name of an object on a piece of paper. He showed the other four sisters the paper. Barrett then asked the first sister to guess the object. Often, the sister named the right object. However, scientists later discovered the sisters cheated. They used signals such as head movements and coughing to communicate with each other.

Zener cards show a star, circle, square, plus sign, or waves.

These signals helped them guess the correct objects.

In the 1930s, American psychologist J.B. Rhine studied ESP at Duke University. Rhine used Zener cards to test ESP. Zener cards have symbols on them. Each card has

During ganzfeld tests, subjects are often placed under red lights. This helps minimize their visual senses.

one of five different symbols. In the tests, a researcher picked a card. The test subject couldn't see the card. The subject then guessed which symbol was on the card. Many people picked the right symbols.

They seemed to be using ESP. They were right more often than could be explained by chance.

Rhine published his research in a book called *Extra-Sensory Perception* in 1934. Rhine's book made more people interested in ESP. He also made the term *ESP* popular. In 1957, Rhine formed the Parapsychological Association. The association's purpose was to study psychic experiences.

In the 1970s, some researchers conducted ganzfeld experiments to test ESP. In these tests, there are two people in different rooms. One person is called the sender. The other is called the receiver. Receivers sit in comfortable chairs and listen to white noise. Their eyes are covered. These conditions help receivers ignore their regular senses. They can focus on extrasensory perception.

The sender is shown an image. The sender tries to telepathically send that image to the receiver. The receiver is shown multiple images and asked to pick the one that was sent. In these studies, receivers were correct more often than could be explained by chance.

The US government asked people with ESP to draw pictures and diagrams of faraway places using clairvoyance.

GOVERNMENT STUDIES

Even the US government wanted to learn

more about ESP. During the 1970s, the US

military spent millions of dollars on ESP

research. The military worked together with

the Stanford Research Institute in California.

Officials wanted to see if ESP could help

Remote viewers tried to use ESP to find missing people and military equipment.

the US military. They wanted to use ESP

to gather **intelligence** during the **Cold**

War. They called their research Project Star

Gate. Annie Jacobsen was a reporter who

wrote about Project Star Gate. She said,

"Scientists would consider, 'Wait a minute, maybe we can read the minds of other government officials; maybe we can see inside a nuclear facility in Russia.'"[3]

For nine years, Angela Ford worked for Project Star Gate. Ford claims to be a medium. She was hired as a remote viewer. Remote viewers used clairvoyance to see faraway locations. Ford's job was to look for missing people. She could find them without leaving the base. "I was good at finding people. I was good at locating things," she said.[4] Project Star Gate ended in 1995.

3
LOOKING AT THE EVIDENCE

Some people are sure that ESP is real. Others say there must be another explanation for premonitions, visions, and paranormal experiences. People on each side have evidence to support their point of view.

PROVING ESP IS REAL

People who believe in ESP say personal accounts are solid evidence. Scientists have also studied ESP in laboratories. Some of their experiments show results that are more than random chance.

Krysia Newman lived in Cambridge, England. She said a dream saved her and

Some people who believe in ESP think there is a paranormal connection between human minds. Others say that empathy explains this connection.

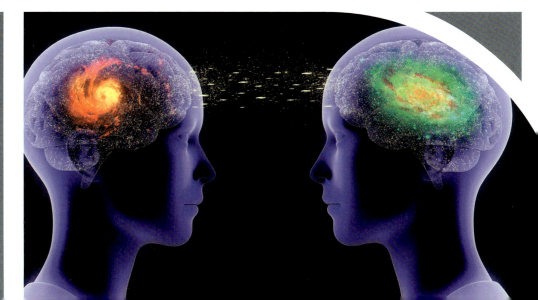

People who believe they have had premonitions often see these visions in their dreams.

her children. Newman had the same dream many times. It was about a pool next to a large hedge. In her dream, a large, black dog jumped out of the hedge. The dog attacked her.

One day, Newman and her children went swimming at a friend's pool. She stood next to a hedge as the children swam. Suddenly a large dog jumped through the hedge. It was just like her dream. She said, "Because of my dream, I felt prepared. I controlled my fear and spoke very calmly to the dog and was amazed when he laid down behind me."[5] Newman believed her dream was a premonition. It could be evidence of ESP.

ESP IN THE LAB

Many scientists have studied ESP in laboratories. They say that some research

Some experiments with Zener cards used machines instead of physical cards.

studies offer evidence of ESP. Some

experiments tested mind reading. J.B.

Rhine's experiments with Zener cards are

an example of this type of research. Each

deck had five kinds of cards. Any person

has a one-in-five chance of guessing the

symbol on a card. But some people did better than that. Some receivers were right more than could be explained by chance.

One leading ESP researcher is Daryl Bem. He tested precognition. In 2011, he published the results of his studies. Bem conducted nine experiments. He said that eight of them showed evidence of ESP.

In one experiment, people studied a long list of words. They had to memorize as many words as possible. Then, they studied a small group of the words. Bem found that participants were better at remembering the words they would later study, even before they studied them. He believed that the participants used precognition to learn from the practice exercises before they happened. Bem later said, "There is evidence for ESP, and I really believe it."[6]

EVIDENCE AGAINST ESP

Some people saw Bem's study as proof of ESP. Others thought the results weren't convincing. Scientists tried to repeat Bem's experiments. Many did not get the same results. They said the failed experiments showed that ESP is not real. James Alcock was a professor of psychology at York

Scientists have tried to recreate Rhine's experiments on clairvoyance. Photographs show subjects being tested for ESP abilities.

University in Toronto. He said, "In science,

if you discover something and claim it as a

fact, then other scientists following similar

The chances of guessing the placement of an image in Bem's study are the same as guessing the result of a flipped coin.

procedures should find the same thing.

[That] never happens with ESP."[7]

Critics also say that the results from

studies of ESP are not that much different

from random chance. In another study,

Bem placed an image behind one of two curtained windows. People picked which window they thought the image was behind. Each person had a 50 percent chance of guessing the correct window. Participants were correct about 53 percent of the time. Bem said they had used ESP.

Critics said it was not much different from picking randomly. Such a small difference is common in ESP research. "If you really have ESP, you should be able to get it right maybe 65 percent, 80 percent of the time," said Jeffrey Rouder, a psychologist at the University of California, Irvine.[8]

Cognitive bias may explain why people believe ESP is real. Cognitive bias happens when people think they see a pattern in a series of random events. For example, a woman sees something that makes her think about her grandmother. Later, her grandmother calls on the phone. Cognitive bias can make the person believe these

A MILLION-DOLLAR PRIZE

Magician James Randi spent many years investigating claims of ESP. He offered a $1 million prize to anyone who could scientifically prove ESP was real. More than 1,000 people tried to claim the prize before the challenge ended in 2015. No one could show strong enough proof to win.

two events are connected. But the woman might say that ESP is involved. She might think she had a premonition of the call.

People also look for evidence to support something they already believe. They might ignore evidence that doesn't support their beliefs. This is called confirmation bias. For example, the woman may ignore the many times she thought about someone and that person did not call.

Some people are sure that ESP is real. Others insist it is not. There is evidence on both sides. The debate keeps people fascinated by ESP.

4

THE CULTURAL IMPACT OF ESP

E SP is part of modern culture all over the world. People with ESP abilities show up in many stories. In everyday life, mediums offer readings. They help people contact the spirits of dead loved ones. In these sessions, people may find their own evidence to decide whether ESP is real.

ESP ON SCREENS

Many movies feature people with ESP.
One famous movie about ESP is *The Sixth Sense* (1999). Malcolm Crowe is a child psychologist. He works with a young boy named Cole Sear. Sear confesses to

People visit psychic mediums all over the world. Psychics offer many kinds of readings.

Crowe that he can see dead people. Sear
explains that he sees spirits walking around
like regular people. The spirits usually do
not know they are dead. They frighten him.
The adults in Sear's life do not believe he
can see dead people. But Crowe eventually
believes the boy. He helps Sear learn to

TELEKINESIS

Telekinesis is the power to move objects with the
mind. Telekinesis is not technically a type of ESP.
However, many people connect these abilities.
Many characters in books, television, and film have
telekinesis. In *Star Wars,* Luke Skywalker learns to
move objects with his mind.

communicate with the spirits so Sear can help them.

ESP also fascinates television audiences. *Stranger Things* is a popular television series on Netflix. It first aired in 2016. One of the show's main characters is Eleven. Eleven has several ESP abilities. She can move objects without touching them. Eleven can also find and communicate with others using her mind. She learns about people by touching items linked to them. In some cases, Eleven can read other people's memories. In the show, Eleven uses her

*Some characters in **Stranger Things** communicate through Christmas lights and a painted alphabet.*

power to save her friends from many

dangerous situations.

Wednesday is another popular television

show. It first streamed on Netflix in 2022.

The show's main character is Wednesday

Addams, who has ESP. Wednesday sees

visions of the past and future.

MEDIUMS AND REALITY TELEVISION

ESP has also been the focus of reality television shows. *Long Island Medium* is a television show about a medium named Theresa Caputo. The show first aired in 2011. Caputo meets with clients and performs psychic readings. She claims to communicate with the dead. She shares these messages with the spirits' loved ones.

While some people are convinced of Caputo's ESP abilities, others are skeptical. A reporter named Victor Fiorillo went to one of Caputo's live readings. He wasn't convinced. "If Caputo really had any special powers . . . her information would be a lot more specific and clear, and she wouldn't be wrong so often," he said.[9] Caputo responds to those who don't believe in her abilities. "I respect that it's hard to understand what I do. Whether someone believes [in ESP], it doesn't matter to me. People believe in what I do," she said.[10] Many people have found peace and acceptance through mediums.

BELIEVERS EVERYWHERE

Millions of Americans believe that ESP is real. Those who believe in ESP have often had a personal experience or know someone who has. Women are also more likely than men to think ESP is real.

Scientists continue to study ESP. Some of them repeat the experiments done by Daryl Bem and J.B. Rhine. Others try new ways to find evidence of ESP. Organizations

ABILITIES OF THE MIND IN BOOKS

In the classic children's book *Matilda*, the main character named Matilda can use telekinesis. The book was written by Roald Dahl and published in 1988. The story follows a young girl. She discovers the ability to move objects with her mind. She uses her power to defend her friends at school and stand up to her unkind parents.

like the Parapsychological Association and the American Society for Psychical Research still exist today. They research the paranormal.

Practices connected with ESP continue to be important all over the world. Many religions and cultures still practice communication with spirits. Others believe in visions of the future. Individuals also talk to psychics and mediums. Whether these experiences are paranormal or not, they are important to many people.

When strange events happen, people look for a way to explain them. In some

BELIEF IN ESP

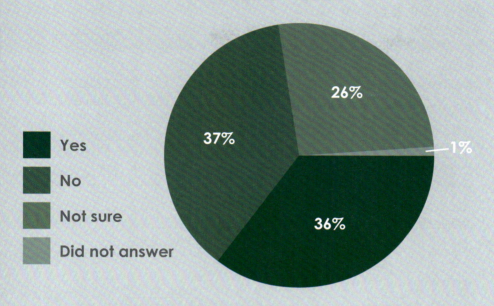

- Yes
- No
- Not sure
- Did not answer

26%

37%

1%

36%

Source: "Do You Believe in Extra-Sensory Perception or E.S.P.?" Statista, January 9, 2023. www.statista.com.

In 2021, Statista asked adults if they believed in ESP. About as many people believe in ESP as people who don't. But many people aren't sure if this phenomenon is real or not.

cases, there is a simple explanation. Other times there is not. Some people believe ESP is the answer. Others think more evidence is needed before they believe ESP is real.

GLOSSARY

coincidences

things that seem connected but happened by chance

Cold War

a period of hostility between the Soviet Union and the United States that lasted from 1947 to 1991

coordinates

a set of numbers used to indicate a specific location

intelligence

information collected by the military about an enemy or location

paranormal

something that is unexplained by science, such as ghosts or aliens

premonition

a strong feeling that something is about to happen

tarot cards

a set of cards used to tell the future

SOURCE NOTES

INTRODUCTION: A PREMONITION OF DISASTER

1. Quoted in Lori Linenberger, "Hyatt Survivor Says Premonition of Disaster Saved Her Life," *UPI*, July 22, 1981. www.upi.com.

CHAPTER ONE: WHAT IS ESP?

2. Quoted in Benjamin Radford, "The Riddle of Twin Telepathy," *Live Science*, March 26, 2018. www.livescience.com.

CHAPTER TWO: THE HISTORY OF ESP

3. Quoted in Kay Lim, "ESP: Inside the Government's Secret Program of Psychic Spies," *CBS News*, March 18, 2018. www.cbsnews.com.

4. Quoted in Lim, "ESP."

CHAPTER THREE: LOOKING AT THE EVIDENCE

5. Quoted in Dr. Julia Mossbridge, "The Scientist Who Says We Can See the Future in Our Dreams," *Daily Mail*, February 20, 2019. www.dailymail.co.uk.

6. Quoted in Ned Potter, "ESP Study Gets Published in Scientific Journal," *ABC News*, January 6, 2011. www.abcnews.go.com.

7. Quoted in Isobel Whitcomb, "What Is ESP?" *Live Science*, August 30, 2021. www.livescience.com.

8. Quoted in Whitcomb, "What Is ESP?"

CHAPTER FOUR: THE CULTURAL IMPACT OF ESP

9. Victor Fiorillo, "I Went to See Long Island Medium Theresa Caputo on Friday Night," *Philadelphia*, July 24, 2017. www.phillymag.com.

10. Quoted in Sierra A. Porter, "The Long Island Medium on Critics, Gifts Ahead of Des Moines Stop," *Des Moines Register*, October 31, 2019. www.desmoinesregister.com.

FOR FURTHER RESEARCH

BOOKS

Megan Borgert-Spaniol, *ESP: Does a Sixth Sense Exist?*
Minneapolis, MN: Abdo, 2019.

Paige V. Polinsky, *ESP*. Minneapolis, MN: Bellwether Media, 2020.

Maddie Spalding, *Ghosts.* San Diego, CA: BrightPoint Press, 2022.

INTERNET SOURCES

"ESP: What Can Science Say?" *Understanding Science*, n.d.
https://undsci.berkeley.edu.

"Extrasensory Perception (ESP)," *Britannica Kids*, n.d.
https://kids.britannica.com.

"Is Telepathy Real?" *Wonderopolis*, n.d. www.wonderopolis.org.

WEBSITES

Live Science: ESP
https://www.livescience.com/ESP

Live Science explores what ESP is and the evidence against it. The website includes links to additional information about ESP studies and other paranormal topics.

Rhine Research Center
www.rhineonline.org/research

The Rhine Research Center conducts research on certain kinds of ESP. Its website includes information about ESP studies and examples of ESP.

Society for Psychical Research: PSI Encyclopedia
https://psi-encyclopedia.spr.ac.uk/

The Society for Psychical Research has a PSI Encyclopedia with information about many types of ESP. The site includes articles about topics such as twin telepathy, lucid dreaming, and ganzfeld tests. It also includes information about many specific paranormal experiences and people with ESP.

INDEX

IMAGE CREDITS

ABOUT THE AUTHOR

Carla Mooney is a graduate of the University of Pennsylvania with a degree in economics. Today, she writes for young people and is the author of many books for young adults and children. Mooney enjoys learning about ESP and other paranormal activity.